WITHDRAWN

American Lives

Paul Revere

Rick Burke

Heinemann Library
Chicago, Illinois

Created by the publishing team
at Heinemann Library

Designed by Sarah Figlio
Photo Research by Dawn Friedman
Printed and Bound in the United States by
Lake Book Manufacturing, Inc.

07 06 05 04 03
10 9 8 7 6 5 4 3 2 1

Library of Congress Cataloging-in-Publication Data
Burke, Rick, 1957-
  Paul Revere / Rick Burke.
     v. cm. — (American lives)
Includes bibliographical references and index.
Contents: Captured — Apollos Rivoire —
Young Paul— Silversmith —Off to war —
Sons of Liberty — Boston Massacre — Boston Tea Party
— Spying — Warning the colonists — Off to war again —
New businesses — Remembering Paul Revere.
  ISBN 1-40340-728-2 (lib. bdg.) — ISBN 1-40343-103-5 (pbk.)
 1. Revere, Paul, 1735-1818—Juvenile literature. 2.
Statesmen—Massachusetts—Biography—Juvenile literature. 3.
Massachusetts—Biography—Juvenile literature. 4.
Massachusetts—History—Revolution, 1775-1783—Juvenile literature.
[1. Revere, Paul, 1735-1818. 2. Statesmen. 3. Silversmiths. 4.
Massachusetts—History—Revolution—1775-1783—Biography.] I. Title.
  F69.R43 B87 2003
  973.3'311'092—dc21
                                          2002154416

Acknowledgments
The author and publishers are grateful to the
following for permission to reproduce copyright
material: Title page, pp. 7, 15 The Granger
Collection; pp. 4, 9, 14, 19, 20, 23, 24, 25 North
Wind Picture Archives; p. 5 Francis G. Mayer/
Corbis; p. 8 Bettmann/Corbis; p. 10 Teapot, Paul
Revere, Jr., Pauline Revere Thayer Collection,
Museum of Fine Arts, Boston; p. 11 Bill Ross/
Corbis; pp. 13, 17 Corbis; p. 16 Sons of Liberty
Bowl, Paul Revere, Jr., Gift by Subscription and
Francis Bartlett Fund, Museum of Fine Arts,
Boston; p. 18 Angelo Hornak/Corbis; pp. 21, 22
Hulton Archive/Getty Images; p. 26 Robert
Holmes/Corbis; p. 27 National Portrait Gallery,
Smithsonian Institution/Art Resource; p. 28 Paul
Revere, Gilbert Stuart, Gift of Joseph W. Revere,
William B. Revere, and Edward H. R. Revere,
Museum of Fine Arts, Boston; p. 29 Art Resource

Cover photograph: The Granger Collection

Special thanks to Patrick Halladay for his help in
the preparation of this book.

Every effort has been made to contact copyright
holders of any material reproduced in this book.
Any omissions will be rectified in subsequent
printings if notice is given to the publisher.

Some words are shown in bold, **like this.** You can
find out what they mean by looking in the glossary.

For more information on the image of Paul Revere that
appears on the cover of this book, turn to page 15.

Contents

Captured

"Stop! If you move another inch, I will shoot you dead!" shouted a British soldier. On the morning of April 19, 1775, British soldiers surrounded Paul Revere.

He tried to outrun the soldiers on his horse, but they cut him off. He tried riding away in a different direction, but they caught him again. The British knew who he was and what he was doing. They were not going to let him carry out his mission.

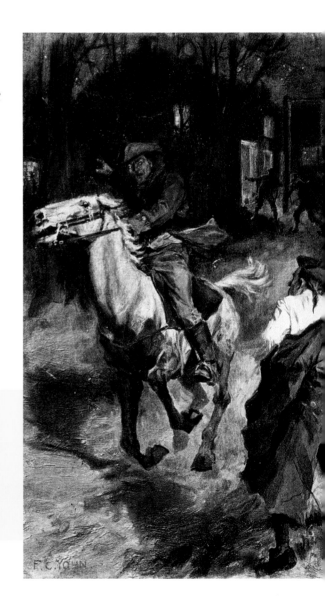

From Boston, Massachusetts, Revere reached Lexington safely. But he was captured on his way to Concord.

The British soldiers were supposed to stop any riders on the roads to the cities of Concord and Lexington in the **colony** of Massachusetts. The British army was marching to those cities from Boston. At the time, Great Britain

In 1931, American artist Grant Wood painted this picture of Revere's ride.

controlled the American colonies. But some people in the colonies were starting to fight to be free from Great Britain's rules.

British soldiers were going to take away any weapons in the Boston area so the colonists could not fight against them. They did not want anyone warning the people there to hide their guns. But they would be too late. Paul Revere had shouted a warning hours before he was caught!

5

Apollos Rivoire

Paul Revere's father, Apollos Rivoire, came to the American **colonies** in 1715. He was thirteen years old. Apollos was born in France. His parents were **Protestants** from France. Most people in France were **Catholic.**

Voyage to America

This map shows France, Great Britain, and the colonies.

Thousands of Protestants left France because they were not being treated well by the Catholics. Apollos's parents wanted Apollos to be free to pray the way he wanted, so they sent him to live with an uncle in Great Britain. The uncle then paid for Apollos to move to Boston in the American colony of Massachusetts.

The Life of Paul Revere

1734	1756	1757	1773
Born in December in Boston.	*Served in the French and Indian War.*	*Married Sarah Orne.*	*Took part in the Boston Tea Party.*

6

The workers in this colonial shop made things from tin in the 1700s.

Apollos was lucky. His uncle paid a man in Boston named John Coney to teach Apollos to be a silversmith. A silversmith is someone who makes things from silver, such as teapots, bracelets, and buttons.

Apollos became Coney's apprentice. An apprentice is a person who works for someone for about seven or eight years until he or she learns everything the person has to show them. Apollos learned a lot from Coney. When he was 21 years old, Apollos opened his own silversmith shop. His customers had trouble saying his name, so Apollos changed it to Paul Revere.

1775	1776	1778–1779	1818
On April 18 and 19, rode to warn other colonists about British soldiers.	Took command of defending the harbor in Boston.	Fought in the **Revolutionary War.**	Died on May 10 in Boston.

Young Paul

Apollos, who was now known as Paul Revere, married Deborah Hitchbourn in the summer of 1729. Her father built boats in Boston. In December 1734, Deborah gave birth to a baby boy. They named the baby Paul. Now, there were two Paul Reveres—Paul Revere the father and Paul Revere the son. Deborah and Paul the father had twelve children, but five of the children died at an early age.

As a boy, Paul loved to watch ships from around the world sail into Boston's harbor. He liked to fly kites in the spring and go sledding down steep hills in the winter.

These are some things that young Paul might have enjoyed doing on a winter day in Boston.

Young and old students were often taught in the same room in the 1700s.

Paul learned his ABCs and how to be polite at a dame school. A dame school was like kindergarten. Paul learned how to read and write at a writing school when he was eight years old. Writing schools were for students who were going to work with their hands or in shops that sold things. Besides learning how to read and write, Paul learned how to add and subtract numbers.

Paul's School

Paul went to the North Writing School on Love Lane in Boston. Writing was taught in one room and reading in another.

Silversmith

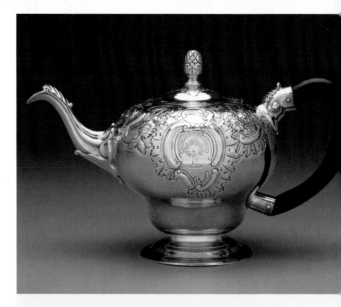

When Paul was thirteen, he became an apprentice in his father's shop. His father was one of the best silversmiths in the **colonies.** Paul's father was a good teacher, and Paul learned a lot.

Paul the son made this silver teapot sometime between 1760 and 1765.

Paul had a gift for making things from metal. He made things from gold, but he worked mostly with silver. Silver cost less to buy and it was easier to get. People in Boston would go to the Revere shop to buy buckles for their shoes and pants, buttons, and teapots and teacups made from silver.

Not all of Paul's time was spent working in his father's shop. When he was fifteen, Paul and his friends got an important job. They were hired to ring the bells in the Old North Church.

By pulling ropes that were tied to the bells, the boys could play songs on the bells. The bells let the people of Boston know a special event was happening. Paul and six friends made their own group. They each signed a paper saying they would practice ringing the bells once a week. They also promised to settle their arguments by voting as a group.

This photo shows what the tower of the Old North Church in Boston looks like today.

Old North Church

The Old North Church is also known as Christ Church. Today, visitors can take tours of the church and see where **lanterns** *were hung to give signals to Paul Revere during the* **Revolutionary War.**

Off to War

Paul's father died in 1752. Paul had learned everything his father had to teach him, but he couldn't own the shop until he was 21. Paul's mother was the owner until he reached that age. Paul's brother Tom, who was fifteen, became his apprentice.

In early 1756, Paul went to fight in a war. The British were fighting the French in North America. Both countries wanted to own land there. Paul joined the British side, but he didn't fight in any battles.

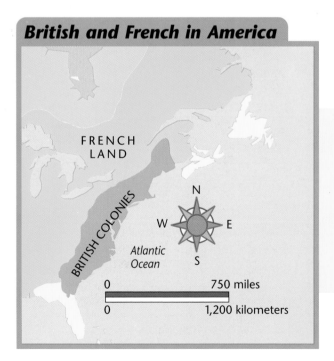

British and French in America

FRENCH LAND

BRITISH COLONIES

Atlantic Ocean

N
W E
S

0   750 miles

0   1,200 kilometers

This map shows the land that the British controlled in green. France controlled the land shown in orange.

The French and Indian War

The war that Paul joined the British army to fight in was called the French and Indian War. Indians also fought for both the French and the British armies.

Paul came back to Boston in November 1756. The same year, he married a 21-year-old woman named Sarah Orne. They had eight children together.

Paul now had a family to feed, but after the war, the people of Boston did not have much money to buy things that Paul made. Paul had to find other ways to make money. He fixed people's teeth and made false teeth. He also taught himself to **engrave** pictures and words. Paul would cut lines into a hard surface and print an image on paper.

Revere made this engraving of British ships in Boston's harbor in 1770.

Sons of Liberty

Great Britain ruled the **colonies.** Some colonists didn't like the way they were being treated by King George III, who ruled Great Britain. They thought it was unfair that they should have to pay taxes and not have a way to help decide what those taxes were.

The taxes were voted on by **Parliament** in London, England, and the colonists had no vote there. The Sons of **Liberty** was a group that was formed in Boston to show the British how much the colonists hated the taxes.

This is what a Sons of Liberty meeting might have looked like.

Paul became a member of the Sons of Liberty. The Sons of Liberty were a secret group. The men talked to each other using a secret code. They also wore special medals around their necks to show each other they belonged to the Sons of Liberty. The medals had a picture of the Liberty Tree.

Artist John Singleton Copley painted this picture of Revere in about 1769.

Paul was one of the leaders of the group. They held their meetings in a place called the Green Dragon Tavern in the north end of Boston.

The Liberty Tree

*In Paul Revere's time, a big elm tree in Boston was called the Liberty Tree. Some people hung **dummies** from the tree that were supposed to look like British tax collectors. They hung them to show that they hated paying taxes.*

Boston Massacre

In 1767, Massachusetts **legislature** members sent a letter to the other legislatures in the colonies. It said the legislatures should oppose paying taxes to Great Britain. This made government leaders in Great Britain angry. They ordered the Massachusetts legislature to take back the letter.

To honor 92 voters in the Massachusetts legislature, Paul made this silver bowl in 1768.

Great Britain's King George III sent an army to Boston to show the colonists he was in charge. But in 1768, by a vote of 92 to 17, the members of the Massachusetts legislature refused to take back the letter.

Townshend Acts

The taxes the colonists didn't want to pay were part of the Townshend Acts. The Townshend Acts were laws that said American colonists had to pay taxes on glass, paper, and tea.

The people of Boston weren't happy about the British army being in their town. Paul had watched British soldiers march into the city. He made an **engraving** of the march. He thought the British soldiers were pushing the colonists around.

Revere made this engraving of the Boston Massacre in 1770.

On March 5, 1770, some men in Boston threw snowballs at British soldiers. The soldiers fired their guns into a crowd and killed five men. The killings became known as the Boston Massacre. Paul Revere made an engraving of this event, too. After the Boston Massacre, all the people of the colonies were angry.

Boston Tea Party

Parliament had put a tax on tea in the **colonies.** This upset the colonists because tea was their favorite drink. They drank it at every meal.

The colonists had fought Parliament's taxes in the past by refusing to use the product that was being taxed, such as paper. Tea was much harder to give up, but Paul's family and thousands of other families decided to do just that. They would quit drinking tea!

Paul Revere owned this house in Boston from 1770 to 1800. It is the oldest building in downtown Boston.

Paul Revere was one of the men who dumped chests of tea into Boston's harbor.

The Sons of **Liberty** decided to show Parliament and the king what they thought about the tax on tea. On the night of December 16, 1773, a group of men in Boston dressed up as Indians. They rowed out to the British ships in the city's harbor.

With axes, they chopped holes in 342 chests of tea and dumped them into the harbor. The group didn't hurt the sailors on the ships, or break anything else, but the tea was ruined. That event became known as the Boston Tea Party.

Spying

King George III told the people of Boston that they would have to pay for the tea that was dumped. He ordered his soldiers to close the harbor in Boston. No boats or ships could enter or leave the harbor. Many people in Boston needed the harbor to be open to make money to buy food and clothes.

This painting shows British soldiers marching into the city of Boston.

Even so, the people of Boston refused to pay for the tea.

Paul began watching to see what the British soldiers were doing. Paul had to be careful not to be caught, because what he was doing was **spying.** At that time, spies were hanged if they were caught.

General Thomas Gage was the leader of the British army. He thought that the **colonists** might attack his soldiers. He wanted to stop that from happening by taking as many guns as possible away from the colonists. Gage and his army took all the guns in Charlestown, which was right across the river from Boston.

Paul heard that Gage planned to march to New Hampshire and take all the guns at a place called **Fort** William and Mary. So, Paul rode his horse all night and warned the colonists there. The colonists hid all of their guns.

This drawing shows Thomas Gage, the British army's leader, in about 1770.

Warning the Colonists

General Gage also wanted to take all the guns in the town of Concord, which was about twelve miles (nineteen kilometers) from Boston. General Gage put soldiers on the roads to stop Paul or others from warning the people in those towns.

The horse that Revere rode was borrowed from Revere's friend John Larkin.

Paul told a man in the Old North Church to hang two **lanterns** in the church's **steeple** if the British were leaving Boston by water and one lantern if they were leaving by land. This would help other people on horses who could see the lanterns leave their towns without being caught. Then, they could warn other people that British soldiers were coming to their towns.

On the night of April 18, 1775, Paul learned the British were marching to Concord and Lexington in Massachusetts. Paul rowed across the Charles River in Boston and borrowed a horse named Brown Beauty.

Revere left Boston at about 10 P.M. and got to Lexington shortly after midnight.

He rode the horse and warned everyone who lived along the road to Lexington that British soldiers were coming.

Paul was caught on his way to Concord. The soldiers let Paul go, but they kept his horse. Because of Paul's warning, the **colonists** of Lexington and Concord were able to get their guns ready to fight the British soldiers. When the colonists and British soldiers fired guns at each other on April 19, 1775, it was the beginning of the **Revolutionary War.**

Paul's Dog

*One old story says that Paul forgot his **spurs** on the night of his ride. He tied a note around his dog's neck and sent it home. The dog came back to Paul later carrying his spurs!*

23

Off to War Again

In 1776, Paul joined the Massachusetts **militia.** His job was to shoot **cannons** at British soldiers in the **Revolutionary War.** Paul really wanted to be in charge of leading other soldiers in the Continental Army.

The Continental Army was made up of men from all over the **colonies,** not just from Massachusetts. General George Washington led this army. When Paul wasn't picked to fight in the Continental Army, he decided to do the best job he could in the militia.

George Washington, shown above, was elected to lead the army on June 15, 1775.

Paul's job was to guard Boston from an attack by British soldiers. Paul and his men went to Castle Island in the city's harbor. If the British came back to Boston, Paul was supposed to stop them with the militia's cannons. The British never came back to Boston. The Americans won the Revolutionary War.

In 1775, cannons captured from the British were moved hundreds of miles to be used in Boston.

During the war, Paul was sent to Maine to help attack a British **fort.** After the battle, other soldiers said that Paul had made mistakes. They made him leave the militia. Paul had to go on **trial** in 1782 to prove that he did not make mistakes. The people who ran the trial were soldiers in charge of leading other soldiers. They found that Paul didn't make mistakes in Maine. He was not guilty.

New Businesses

After the **Revolutionary War,** Paul wanted to do more than make beautiful things from silver. He and his sons started some other businesses. One of them was a bell-making business.

This bell made by Revere is kept in a museum in Boston.

In 1792, the bell in the Second Church of Boston cracked. Paul said he could make a new one. He studied other church bells and thought he could do it. He melted down the copper from the old bell and used some different metals, too. The new bell sounded great!

Paul's Bells

Paul and his sons made more than 100 church bells. Twenty-three are still ringing today. One of them is in King's Chapel in Boston. Paul said that bell was the best-sounding bell he and his sons ever made.

Old Ironsides

One of the ships that used Paul's copper sheets was the American ship called the USS Constitution. *During a battle in 1812 against Great Britain, British* **cannonballs** *bounced off the sides of the ship. It was given the nickname "Old Ironsides." The ship is now a museum in Boston's harbor.*

Paul also started a business that is still around, almost 200 years after his death. Paul used heavy rollers to press copper into big sheets. He sold the sheets to the United States Navy. The navy nailed the sheets to the bottoms of ships to make the ships stronger. Paul also made brass and copper nails and bolts that were used on the ships. Paul made the copper sheets that were put on the dome of the Massachusetts **capitol** in Boston.

Paul Revere is seen here in an **engraving** from 1801. In December 1801, Revere would have been 67 years old.

Remembering Paul Revere

Paul died on May 10, 1818. He was remembered in Boston for the things he did to help make the United States a free country. But he was not well known in the rest of the country. That changed about 50 years after Paul died. A poet named Henry Wadsworth Longfellow wrote about Paul's ride on April 18, 1775. The poem was read and memorized by schoolchildren across the United States.

Artist Gilbert Stuart painted this picture of Revere in 1813, five years before Revere's death.

"Paul Revere's Ride"

Longfellow's poem "Paul Revere's Ride" was written in 1863, 85 years after Paul's ride to warn Lexington and Concord. Longfellow's grandfather was one of the soldiers who said Paul had made mistakes in Maine.

This statue of Revere is near the Old North Church in Boston.

Millions of Americans learned about Paul Revere's ride from Longfellow's poem. Paul Revere risked his life a number of times riding from Boston to let other **colonists** know what was happening. But that is not the only thing for which Paul Revere is remembered. He is also remembered because he was a successful American businessperson who tried new things, such as being a dentist, rolling copper sheets, and making bells.

Glossary

cannon large gun from which large metal balls called cannonballs are shot

capitol building where a legislature meets

Catholic Christian who belongs to the church and religion led by the pope

colony group of people who moved to another land but who are still ruled by the country they moved from. People who live in a colony are called colonists.

dummy pieces of clothing filled with paper or other stuffing to look like a human body

engrave to carve letters or designs on stone, wood, or metal

fort building with strong walls and guns to defend against attacks from enemies

lantern case that protects a light from rain or wind

legislature group of elected people who make, change, or get rid of laws

liberty condition of being independent, or free from the control of others

militia soldiers called to fight in an emergency

Parliament group of people who make the laws for Great Britain and its colonies

Protestant Christian who is not a member of the Catholic Church

Revolutionary War war from 1775 to 1783 in which the American colonists won freedom from Great Britain

spur metal worn on a boot used to make horses move faster

spy to secretly watch or follow someone

steeple church tower

trial hearing in a court of law to decide whether a charge or claim is true or to settle a problem or disagreement

More Books to Read

Ford, Carin T. *Paul Revere: Patriot.* Berkeley Heights, N.J.: Enslow Publishers, Inc., 2003.

Santore, Charles. *Paul Revere's Ride.* New York: HarperCollins Children's Book Group, 2003.

Sutcliffe, Jane. *Paul Revere.* Minneapolis, Minn.: Lerner Publishing Group, 2002.

Places to Visit

Paul Revere House
19 North Square
Boston, Massachusetts 02113
Visitor Information: (617) 523-2338

Old North Church (Christ Church)
193 Salem Street
Boston, Massachusetts 02113-1198
Visitor Information: (617) 523-4848

Index